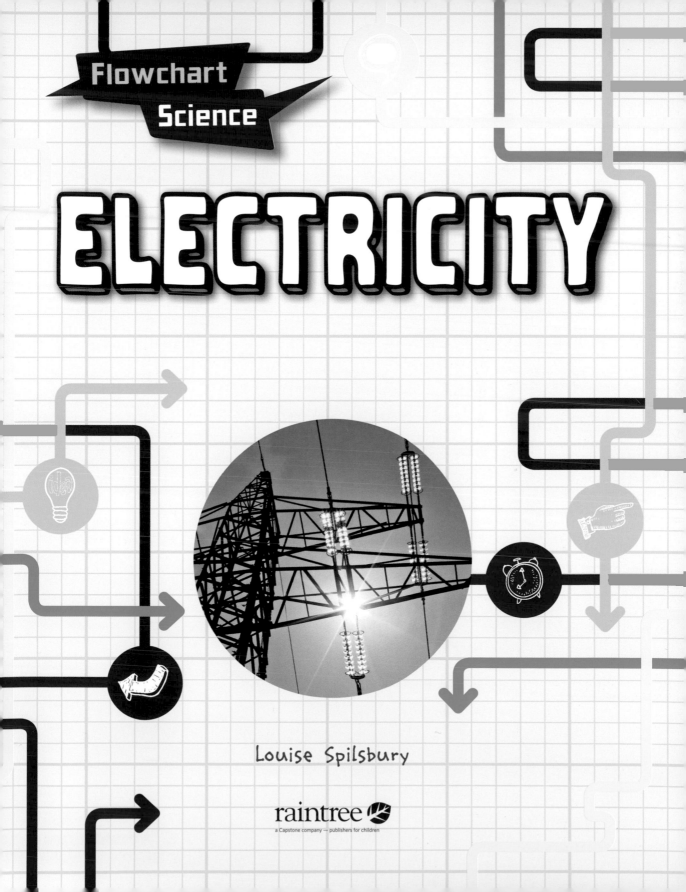

Flowchart
Science

ELECTRICITY

Louise Spilsbury

raintree
a Capstone company — publishers for children

Raintree is an imprint of Capstone Global Library Limited, a company incorporated in England and Wales having its registered office at 264 Banbury Road, Oxford OX2 7DY – Registered company number: 6695582

www.raintree.co.uk
myorders@raintree.co.uk

Produced for Raintree by Calcium
Edited by Sarah Eason and Amanda Learmonth
Designed by Simon Borrough
Picture research by Susannah Jayes
Production by Victoria Fitzgerald
Originated by Capstone Global Library Ltd © 2016
Printed and bound in China

ISBN 978 1 4747 3127 0
20 19 18 17 16
10 9 8 7 6 5 4 3 2 1

British Library Cataloguing in Publication Data
A full catalogue record for this book is available from the British Library

Acknowledgements
We would like to thank the following for permission to reproduce photographs:
Shutterstock: Alisalipa 28–29, Constantine Androsoff 14t, Art of Sun 8–9, Atomazul 19r, Marcel Clemens 13t, Daxiao Productions 38–39, Everett Historical 6b, Freedom Studio 33tr, Peter Gudella 32–33, Gyn9037 4–5, Nir Levy 6–7, Soloviova Liudmyla 44–45, Liunian 22b, Lzf 34–35, Meryll 12–13, Stuart Monk 39tr, Nenetus 29, William Perugini 26–27, Lisa S. 1, 21r, Ssuaphotos 14–15, 40–41, Taddeus 18–19, Luisma Tapia 27tr, Stephen VanHorn 23, Xfox01 15r, Yellowj 20–21.

Cover art reproduced with permission of: Shutterstock: Denkcreative, Lineartestpilot.

Every effort has been made to contact copyright holders of material reproduced in this book. Any omissions will be rectified in subsequent printings if notice is given to the publisher.

Contents

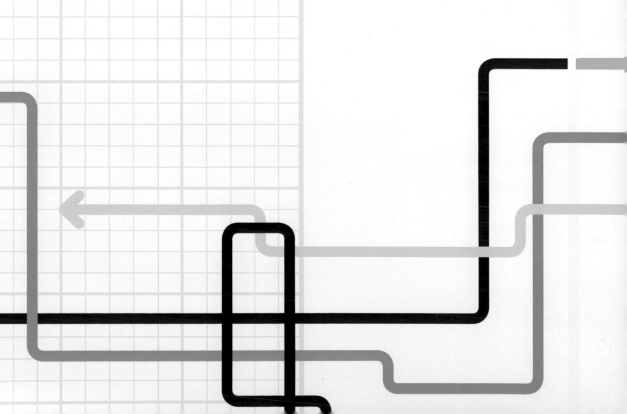

Chapter 1
What is electricity?

We take electricity for granted. We simply flick a switch and lights come on or music plays. We might not think about electricity much, but our lives would be very different without it.

Electricity is the **energy** that is used to power most of the machines that you use every day. Tiny batteries supply electrical energy to watches and calculators, and power lines bring electricity to our homes to run our televisions, DVD players, computers, freezers and washing machines. Electricity even powers motors that make cars, buses, trains and ships move. We cannot see electricity, but we witness its power when it makes things work.

We would not be able to see well in our cities at night without electricity to power lights on streets, cars and buildings.

Electricity is the flow of moving **electrons**. **Atoms** are the building blocks of all matter. Everything around us is made up of atoms, but they are so tiny that we cannot see them even with a regular microscope. There are more than 100 different kinds of atoms and these combine in different ways to make everything in the universe. Electrons are tiny particles that zoom around the centre of an atom at incredible speeds. Sometimes electrons escape from one atom and join another atom. When electrons move between atoms, they carry electrical energy from one place to another. This energy is electricity.

Get smart!

All substances are made of atoms, from stars to sea stars, water to walls, the air above Earth and even us! They are so incredibly small that millions of them would fit on the head of a pin. The human body is made up of 7 billion billion billion atoms!

Static electricity

The type of electricity we use to power machines is called "**current** electricity" because it moves from place to place. There is another kind of electricity: **static electricity**. When something is static it barely moves. Static electricity is a type of electricity that builds up in one place. When enough static electricity builds up, it jumps from one material to another as a spark of current electricity. It can create dramatic effects, such as bolts of lightning.

Static electricity is created when certain materials are rubbed together. Lightning happens when minuscule pieces of ice blown around inside storm clouds rub together over and over. The **friction** between them causes electrons to move between atoms, and this can create sparks that suddenly flash towards Earth. These lightning bolts are extremely hot.

You have probably felt static electricity yourself. Have you ever rubbed a balloon on your hair to make it stand on end? When you rub a balloon on your hair, static electricity pulls up the strands of hair. The balloon also becomes **charged** with static electricity and may stick to a wall or ceiling.

In 1752, Benjamin Franklin famously experimented with the electricity in lightning.

Get smart!

American scientist Benjamin Franklin wanted to prove that lightning was a form of electricity. He flew a kite in a thunderstorm, which is something you should never try yourself. During the storm, electricity flowed down the kite string into a metal key that Franklin was holding. The spark of static electricity that passed into his hand gave Franklin a slight **electric shock**.

When you take off a woolly hat, static electricity can make your hair stand on end.

How electricity works

We have seen what electricity can do, but exactly how does electricity occur? What makes electrons move from atom to atom?

Atoms are made up of three different types of particles: **protons**, **neutrons** and electrons. Protons and neutrons form the centre, or **nucleus**, of an atom and they do not move. Electrons are smaller than protons and neutrons and they are not part of the nucleus. They move around and around the nucleus very quickly, in a similar way to planets moving around the Sun. Neutrons have no electrical charge, protons have a positive charge and electrons have a negative charge. Usually, an atom has an equal number of protons and electrons, so they are in balance and the atom has no overall electrical charge.

When objects rub together, like a balloon and your hair, the energy from your moving hand causes some of the electrons to be knocked out of the atoms that make up the balloon. The balloon atoms now have more protons than electrons, so the balloon has a slight positive charge. The extra electrons collect on your hair, so it has more electrons and therefore a slight negative charge. Just as with **magnets**, opposite charges attract, so your negatively charged hair is pulled towards the positively charged balloon by static electricity. When electrons move, they become current electricity and carry electrical energy from one place to the next.

Get smart!

Electrons travel around the nucleus of an atom at speeds of about 2,250 kilometres (1,400 miles) per hour. At that speed, an electron could travel around Earth in just over 18 seconds!

This is a simple model of an atom to help you understand how an atom is structured. The pathways around the central nucleus represent the moving electrons.

How electrons flow

Take a look at this flowchart to understand how electrons flow.

An energy **source**, such as light, heat or a **chemical reaction**, knocks an electron from an atom.

In this way, electrons are bumped from atom to atom. As an atom gains an electron, it releases another electron, making the next atom negatively charged. That atom releases an electron, and so on, and so on.

When electrons move, the current can flow through an electrical system.

All atoms want to be balanced (have the same number of protons and electrons), so this sets off a chain reaction.

The free electron that has been knocked off the first atom moves torwards a new atom. The second atom now has an extra electron and is negatively charged.

The negatively charged atom wants to restore balance. It releases an electron, which moves to the next atom.

Flowchart
Smart

Making electricity

The electricity we use in our homes, schools and other buildings, by plugging computers and other appliances into electric sockets, is made in power plants. Many power plants burn **fossil fuels**, such as coal, to produce the energy needed to create electricity.

Energy is amazing. It can never be made or destroyed, but it can be changed from one form to another. For example, when we run, the chemical energy we get from food turns into **kinetic** (movement) and thermal (heat) energy. In a power plant, energy is changed from one form to another, too. When different fuels are burnt, the chemical energy stored inside them changes into heat energy, and this heat energy is used to make electrical power.

The heat energy in power plants is used to boil water and produce steam, in the same way that steam is produced when a kettle boils. This steam is funnelled towards the blades of a **turbine**, which is like a big fan. The steam causes the turbine to spin, turning heat energy into kinetic energy. The spinning turbine rotates coils of wire surrounded by big **magnets** in a **generator**. These magnets create strong pulling forces, and as the wires spin between the magnets, electrons in the wire are forced to move between atoms. Kinetic energy has turned into electrical energy, and an electric current begins to flow through the wire.

Nuclear power plants use uranium as the energy source for creating electricity. Uranium is a very heavy radioactive metal.

These large cooling towers are releasing steam into the air at a nuclear power station.

Get smart!

All power plants create heat to boil water, make steam and spin turbines. Some power plants burn natural gas, others burn coal. A nuclear power station creates heat by splitting apart atoms of uranium, a special type of metal.

Renewable power

Coal, oil and gas are called fossil fuels because they take millions of years to form from the remains of living things deep underground. Fossil fuels are also called non-renewable fuels because they take so long to form, and once they are gone we cannot replace them. As demand for electricity grows, many people believe that we should be increasing our use of renewable forms of energy, because they can be reused and replaced.

Wind power is the fastest-growing source of electricity in the world.

Hydroelectric power stations use the energy of falling water to make electricity.

There are several different types of **renewable energy**. Biomass energy is generated from plant or animal waste or material, ranging from maize husks (plants' dry outer coverings) to camel dung. These materials originally obtained their energy from the Sun. Biomass fuel is burnt to provide heat energy that can be converted into electricity. In a hydroelectric power plant, water is stored behind a dam and when released through pipes, it turns a turbine. The turbine is connected to a generator, which produces electricity. A wind farm uses the energy of the wind to spin the blades of the turbine.

Solar or photovoltaic cells are devices that change sunlight energy directly into electricity. When light hits thin wafers of silicon contained within the cells, it makes a very small electric current flow between the layers of silicon. Metal strips on top of the solar cell carry the electricity away from the silicon layers to wires, and the wires take the electric current to wherever it is needed. Individual solar cells are often connected together in solar panels to generate larger amounts of power.

Energy from the Sun can be used to generate solar power.

Get flowchart smart!

How power plants work

Learn how power plants produce electricity by following the flowchart.

A fuel such as coal, gas or oil is burnt to provide heat.

Heat from the burning fuel is used to boil water in a boiler.

Steam from the boiling water rises upwards into turbines.

The pressure or pushing force of the steam provides kinetic energy to turn the blades of the turbines.

The movement of the turbines turns a magnet in a generator, which produces electricity.

Flowchart Smart

Chapter 3
Electricity on the move

Electricity produced in power plants is carried along metal cables and wires to homes, factories, offices and other places where people need it. We use metals to carry electricity because metal is a good **conductor** of electricity. Metal allows electricity to flow through it easily.

Electricity travels through some materials better than others. Materials that are made up of atoms whose electrons move easily are good conductors of electricity. Iron and lead are good conductors of electricity, but one of the best conductors is copper. Metals such as copper have electrons that are not linked tightly to their atoms. These loose electrons move freely and this creates an electric current. Copper is used to make electricity cables, and it also forms part of the pins of a plug.

Other materials conduct electricity, too. Graphite, which is used to make some pencil leads, conducts electricity. Water can also conduct electricity. Although water is a poor conductor compared to metal, it can still conduct enough electricity to be dangerous. That is why you should always dry your hands before you touch anything electrical. If you touch an electric switch with wet hands, the water could conduct the electricity to your body and give you an electric shock.

Copper wires are twisted together in a cable. The copper is covered with a plastic coating.

Get smart!

In the past, tall buildings could ignite if they were struck by a bolt of lightning. Today, most tall buildings have lightning conductors on top of them. These are metal rods connected to long wires that conduct the lightning's electricity into the ground and keep the building safe.

Lightning is hitting the lightning conductor on top of this tall tower.

19

Insulators

It is important to use good conductors of electricity to carry electricity as efficiently as possible. It is equally important to know which materials can prevent electricity from flowing out of metal cables or wires and being wasted, or even causing injury. Materials that do not conduct electricity well or stop the flow of electricity are called **insulators**.

Insulators are materials made up of atoms that hold their electrons very tightly. This means that electrons do not move through them very well. We use the word **resistance** to describe how well a material prevents, or resists, the flow of a current of electricity. Conductors are materials that have a low resistance. Insulating materials do not let electricity flow, so they have a high resistance. Most materials other than metals do not conduct electricity well. The best insulators include rubber, plastic, cloth, glass and dry air. In rubber, the electrons are very tightly bound, so electricity does not flow through rubber at all.

We use insulators in different ways. Metal wires are usually covered in plastic to make sure the electric current only flows along the wire. On electricity pylons, glass discs are often used to prevent the electricity that flows through metal power lines from flowing down the pole to the ground. Plugs and sockets in homes are covered with plastic or rubber for protection. If you use an electric toothbrush, notice how it is covered with plastic to stop your damp fingers from touching the metal parts inside that could conduct electricity to your body.

Electricians wear insulating gloves and use insulated tools to protect themselves.

The insulating glass discs on this pylon prevent electricity from entering the pylon itself.

From power plants to us

Most electricity is generated in large power plants far away from towns and cities, and carried to homes, offices and factories through a huge network of wires and cables. Electricity may have to travel hundreds of kilometres before people use it, and it must go through different machines to ensure it ends up where it is needed. Together, the power plants, wires and cables, and machines that deliver our electrical power are known as the National Grid.

When electricity leaves a power plant it flows into a machine called a **transformer**. The transformer increases the **voltage** to push the electricity over long distances. Voltage is the pushing force that moves electricity through a wire. The electricity flows through thick metal cables called transmission lines. These are buried safely underground or strung between pylons that carry the cables high above the ground.

The flow of electricity from power plants is controlled inside a substation.

When the wires arrive at a town or city, they pass into a substation. Inside the substation there are more transformers. These transformers lower the voltage so the electric current can travel safely along smaller power lines. From the substation, the electricity travels through more overhead or underground transmission lines to your street. There, small transformers on top of electricity poles reduce the voltage further.

This process ensures that electricity comes into homes and other buildings at a safe voltage for people to use. The wires that carry electricity into buildings usually flow through a meter. These meters measure how much electricity people use, so the power company knows what to charge them. From the meter box, wires run through the walls of a building to sockets and plugs, so we can use electricity to power lights and other appliances.

Wall sockets let electricity flow through an appliance's cord when we plug it in.

Get flowchart smart!

How electricity travels

Follow the flowchart to see how electricity travels from its source to your home.

→ A power plant uses turbines and generators to generate electric current.

Cables carry the electricity to a transformer.

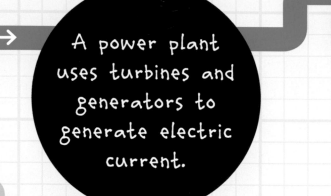

As electricity enters a home it goes through a meter that measures how much electricity that home uses.

Transformers on top of poles in the street reduce the voltage again and pass the electricity along wires towards homes.

The transformer increases the voltage to push the electricity along transmission lines towards towns and cities.

As transmission lines approach towns and cities, transformers inside a substation lower the voltage.

The lower-voltage electric current flows along more transmission lines to streets.

Flowchart Smart

Electric currents only flow if they are in a **circuit**. A circuit is a pathway or loop made of wires around which an electric current flows. Imagine an athlete running around a circular racetrack. If there were a wide crack halfway around the track, the runner would have to stop and could not go any further. It's the same for an electric current. It needs a continuous path through which to flow.

Get smart!

Switches control the flow of electricity. A lamp switch has two metal strips separated by a spring. When the switch is turned on, the metal strips are pushed together, and the circuit is completed. The electric current flows, and the lamp lights up. When the switch is turned off, the pressure is taken off, the spring releases the metal strips, and it makes a gap in the circuit. The electric current cannot flow, and the lamp switches off.

Relay runners pass a baton to each other as they complete a lap in a race. Electrons move from atom to atom around an unbroken circuit in a similar way.

When we switch on a lamp or television, the switch completes the circuit so that electricity begins to flow through the metal conductor inside the wire or cable to the appliance and it turns on. Next, the electricity flows through the cable to the socket in the wall in one unbroken path to complete its loop. If there is a break in the circuit, electricity cannot flow. If a wire breaks, the television will not work. Switches work in a similar way, by breaking or completing a circuit.

It is important to be able to turn machines on and off when they are not needed. Turning appliances off saves energy and lengthens the life of the appliance.

The lines on this electrical circuit board are the paths along which electrons flow.

People can change circuits to allow them to be used in different ways or to solve different challenges. Circuits can be changed by using wires of different widths, or by adding extra loops of wire.

A string of Christmas lights is an example of a series circuit. In a series circuit, there is only one path of wire from the power source through all the loads (the things that use the electricity) and back to the source. This means that all the current in the circuit must flow through all the loads until it gets back to the power source. In this set-up, if one bulb breaks or is removed, the circuit is broken and all the lights go out.

The electricity in our homes has wires set up in a parallel circuit. There are extra wires coming off the main circuit that run to different sockets in different rooms. The current splits as it reaches the place where each new loop is added, so the current flows around all the loops. Each loop has its own switch so that we can turn individual sockets off without breaking the circuit.

Christmas lights are usually wired in a series circuit.

If you change the thickness of the wires in a circuit, you change how quickly the electricity can flow through it. It's a little like comparing a single lane road to a motorway with several lanes. More cars can travel along the wider road at one time than along a single lane. Because thinner wires resist the flow of electricity, we say they have a higher resistance than thicker wire. Changing the resistance of a wire changes the current, and this can be very useful. People use resistance to make light switch dimmers and volume controls on electronic devices.

Mobile phones contain a small but complex circuit board that makes them work.

Get flowchart smart!

How circuits work

Find out how circuits work by following this flowchart.

A battery or other power source creates the voltage (force) that makes electrons move from atom to atom.

The electric current moves through a wire that forms a continuous loop or path.

The electric current goes back to the power source, where the voltage can force the electrons out again.

When the wire reaches a device like a lamp, the electric current passes through wires inside it and gives it the power to make it work.

Then the electric current continues along the pathway of wires.

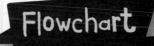
Flowchart

Smart

Chapter 5
Batteries

We plug many of our appliances into a wall socket to connect them to the electricity supply. However, what happens when you want to use a machine on the go, to listen to music on the way to school or to power a torch when you are out walking in the dark? Batteries can be used to produce small amounts of electricity that power small machines or gadgets that we want to carry with us.

The positive ends of these batteries are clearly marked with a "+" symbol.

Get smart!

Batteries come in a variety of shapes and sizes. Some are as big as a brick. Others can be smaller than a coin. Batteries are different sizes because they have different voltages. To get the right amount of power you need for different devices, you can buy different batteries or use more than one battery. It's important to use the correct battery for every device, or it won't work correctly.

This mobile phone battery slots into the back of the phone.

If a device, such as a torch, needs more than one battery, it's important that you put the batteries in correctly so that they connect to make a complete circuit. Take a look at a battery. You will see that each one has two **terminals**. These are the points on a battery from which electricity comes out and returns. One terminal is positive and marked with a "+" sign, and the other is negative and marked with a "−" sign. You must insert the batteries so that the electric current flows from the negative terminal of one battery to the positive terminal of another to complete a circuit. If you put the batteries in the wrong way around, the machine simply won't work!

Battery power

A battery is not a small store of electricity. Instead, a battery contains chemicals that react together to produce electricity. A battery can sit in a drawer for a year and still be ready to work. It only starts to use up energy when you connect it in a circuit and electrons begin to flow. When you turn on a torch, the energy stored in the chemicals inside the battery makes electricity light the bulb.

Lithium-ion batteries inside mobile phones supply electricity to power the phone.

Get smart!

Batteries contain chemicals that can be hazardous if not used and disposed of correctly, so always handle them and recycle them carefully. Never put batteries in your mouth or anywhere other than where they are stored or used.

When we put the batteries into a machine and turn it on, a chemical reaction takes place in the battery. Loose electrons from chemicals in the battery leave the chemicals and create an electric current. The electrons flow from the first battery into a wire, and they flow from the negative to the positive terminal of any other batteries. They need a complete circuit for the chemical reaction to take place.

Batteries stop working when the chemicals inside them can no longer complete a chemical reaction and release electrons. When rechargeable batteries stop working, we can use battery chargers to return electrons to the chemicals so the batteries can be used again. Cars use huge batteries to provide a spark of electricity to help start the engine. Chemical reactions happen efficiently in the acid inside rechargeable batteries so that when we recharge a car battery, it is as good as new. Car batteries can be used for years before they need to be replaced.

Get flowchart smart!

How batteries work

Find out how batteries create electricity and work in a circuit using this flowchart.

Chemicals inside a battery react with each other to release loose electrons.

Electric current from the battery flows through the wire and passes through a load, such as a bulb, to make a device like a torch work.

The electric current returns to the battery.

The battery is placed into a device and the switch turned to the "on" position to complete a circuit.

When a wire connects both ends of the battery, the electrons can flow. The chemical energy starts changing to electrical energy.

Flowchart Smart

Chapter 6
Using electricity

Electricity is useful to us because it can be turned into other forms of energy, such as heat, light, sound and motion. We change electrical energy into other forms of energy to light our streets, heat our homes and play music.

Inside a hairdryer there is a coil of thin, high-resistance wire. Behind this coil is a small fan. When you turn on the hairdryer, some of the electric energy is changed into kinetic energy to make the blades of the fan turn. This sends cool air out of the dryer nozzle. As electric current passes through the high-resistance wire, it slows down, and when this happens some of the electrical energy is converted into heat. As the air from the fan passes through the hot coil of metal wire, it heats up and the warm air dries your hair.

As electric current passes through the high-resistance wires inside some light bulbs, the wires glow, producing light and heat.

Sound is also a type of energy. Microphones change sound energy into a form of electrical energy. This allows the sounds to be played louder through a loudspeaker, which is a machine that converts electric signals back into sounds.

Electricity powers the turntables to spin these records. Resistance devices control the volume and electrically powered loudspeakers make sure everyone can hear the music.

In a neon sign, electricity is converted to light energy.

Get smart!

A volume control on a music player allows us to control how loud sound is when it leaves a loudspeaker. Moving the volume control changes the length of a resistance wire. A slider inside the volume control makes the electric current travel along a longer or shorter distance of wire. Making the current travel further increases the resistance and lowers the volume.

Electromagnets

Electricity can be used to create an **electromagnet**. Electromagnets are in many of the objects we use every day. There are electromagnets in the motors that turn blades in electric mixers or the drums inside washing machines, and there are electromagnets in loudspeakers. Salvage yards use strong electromagnets to lift and drop old cars and other metal objects.

When an electric current flows through a wire, it creates a weak **magnetic field** around the wire. A magnetic field is an area in which the invisible pulling or pushing force of a magnet can be felt. If you wind the wire around an iron core or rod to make a tight coil, you create a much larger magnetic force when you run an electric current through the wire. This creates a stronger electromagnet.

Electromagnets are used in many devices, from simple doorbells to amazing maglev trains, which hover at high speed above the tracks. When you press a doorbell, an electromagnet attracts a metal lever that hits a bell or buzzer. When you release the switch, the current stops flowing, the electromagnet stops working and the doorbell stops ringing.

Every magnet has one end that can attract and one end that can repel, or push away, other magnets. Maglev trains have electromagnets under the carriages that repel electromagnets on the train track, making the train hover above the track. Normally, there is friction between a train's wheels and the track, but there is no friction with a maglev train.

The fastest maglev trains travel at speeds of more than 600 km (370 mi.) per hour.

Get flowchart smart!

How doorbells work

Follow the flowchart for a closer look at electromagnets in doorbells.

Pressing a doorbell completes an electrical circuit.

An electric current flows through the circuit and passes through a wire coiled tightly around a metal core. This turns the coil of wire into an electromagnet.

The electromagnet is turned off and the metal lever moves back into position, ready to move again the next time someone presses the doorbell.

The electromagnet creates a magnetic field.

The electromagnet's magnetic force attracts a metal lever.

The lever hits a bell and makes it ring.

Once the lever is out of position, the electric circuit is broken.

Flowchart Smart

Electricity and us

Electricity is a vital source of power that we use every day in many ways. Around the world, more and more people are using increasing numbers of electric devices and electricity, and there is concern that fossil fuels will run out. Burning fossil fuels in power plants also releases gases into the air that trap more of the Sun's warmth on Earth. This is causing **climate change**. In the future, we are likely to see increased use of renewable energy sources.

It is important to save electricity whenever you can. Cutting down on electricity usage helps the environment and saves you and your family money. It is easy to do. You can choose to buy machines that are designed to use less energy. You can close windows and doors to prevent heat escaping and reduce wasted energy. Make sure you turn off lights, televisions and other electrical appliances when you leave a room or when you are not using them. Turn off devices completely because when you leave them on standby, they continue to use a small amount of electricity. Turning equipment off at the plug can save energy and money.

Get smart!

Electricity is a very safe form of energy as long as it is used correctly. If not, it can give you a nasty and dangerous electric shock. So, remember: never fly kites near power lines, never climb trees near electricity pylons or other overhead transmission lines, and never touch anything electrical with wet hands or take electrical appliances into the bathroom.

Fly kites in open spaces, never near power lines.

45

Glossary

atom the smallest particle of a substance that can exist by itself

charged having electricity in it

chemical reaction process in which atoms in two or more substances react with each other and form new substances

circuit complete pathway or loop through which an electric current flows

climate change process in which the environment changes to become warmer or cooler, drier or wetter over a period of time

conductor material that allows electricity to move through it easily

current steady flow of electrons

electric shock jolt of electric energy that can hurt or even kill an animal or person

electromagnet object that becomes magnetic when an electric current is passed through it

electron negatively charged particle that whirls around the nucleus of an atom

energy ability or power to do work

fossil fuel fuel formed from the remains of ancient living things; fossil fuels include oil, coal and gas

friction force occurring when two surfaces rub against each other

generator machine that creates electricity by turning a magnet inside a coil of wire

insulator material that slows or stops electricity moving through it

kinetic to do with movement

magnetic field space around a magnetic object in which magnetic forces can be felt

magnet piece of material, usually metal, that can attract iron or steel

neutron particle in the nucleus of an atom that has no electric charge

nucleus centre of an atom, made up of neutrons and protons

proton positively charged particle in the nucleus of an atom that does not move

renewable energy electricity made from a source that can be replaced or used again

resistance measure of how an object restricts the flow of current

silicon chemical element found within Earth

source person or thing from which something comes

static electricity electricity that collects on the surface of something and does not flow

terminal positive or negative connection point on a battery

transformer device that increases or reduces voltage of an electric current

turbine machine with blades that can be used to generate electricity

voltage force of an electrical current

Find out more

Books

Electricity (Eyewitness), DK Editors (Dorling Kindersley, 2013)

Electricity and Magnetism (Mind Webs), Anna Claybourne (Wayland, 2016)

Energy (Earth Cycles), Jillian Powell (Franklin Watts, 2014)

Shocking Electricity (Horrible Science), Nick Arnold (Scholastic Children's Books, 2014)

Websites

Find out more about electricity at:
www.bbc.co.uk/guides/z96ckqt

Learn about the ways in which we can generate electrical energy:
www.childrensuniversity.manchester.ac.uk/ interactives/science/energy/electricity/

Read all about electrical circuits here:
www.dkfindout.com/uk/science/electricity/circuits/

Discover more about how to use electricity safely at:
powerup.ukpowernetworks.co.uk/powerup/en/ under-11/

Index